DIRECTORY

OF

AMERICAN PRESIDENTS

George Washington to George Walker Bush

Publisher: Yuksel Atillasoy

Woodside House

Text copyright 2001 by Yuksel Atillasoy
www.woodsidehouse.net

This book may be ordered by mail from the publisher
Woodside House
P.O. Box 750217
Forest Hills, N.Y. 11375

Library of Congress Cataloging-in-Publication Data
LCCN 2001094096
Directory of American Presidents compiled and published by Yuksel Atillasoy

Includes bibliographical references

Publisher's note : This single volume directory is a compilation of data about 43 U.S. Presidents, their
wives, children, birth and death dates , location, party, term, education, occupation and notable events.
Numerous books have been published about the presidents. This directory includes statistics, such as
the states they were from, colleges attended, occupation and first names. It also includes the inauguration
oath of office, a photograph of President George Washington's Inauguration, famous speeches and
illustrations.

ISBN:0-9712353-0-9
Publisher Yuksel Atillasoy
Published by Woodside House
For Information about other publications please visit us
on the web
www.woodsidehouse.net

All copyright requests for any part of this work should be emailed to
woodsidehouse@prodigy.net
cover by: c.are. Brooklyn, NYC

Printed in United States
First edition

ACKNOWLEDGMENTS

I would like to thank Maribel Soto for her efforts in the physical preparation of the manuscript and illustrations, my friend Professor Alexander Bardosh, and Ms. Jaime Burton for proofreading. I am most indebted to my wife Ilkin for her help in publishing this book.

PREFACE

I dedicate this book DIRECTORY OF AMERICAN PRESIDENTS to my parents and family.

At a very young age I became interested in the history and lives of the American Presidents. I believe this to be an appropriate time to initiate my grandchildren into the challenges and pleasures of learning history. It is my sincere hope that my grandchildren, readers, trivia and game show contestants will share my fascination with American History.

DIRECTORY OF AMERICAN PRESIDENTS is a compilation of data of the 43 U.S. Presidents from George Washington to George Walker Bush. It includes information about their wives, parents, children, party, term, religion and education. This directory is not intended to be an inclusive or comprehensive review of American Presidents. It is intended to function as a source of quick reference, offering brief data on important events and terms of service for each of the U. S. Presidents.

On September 11, 2001 while this book was being printed, terrorists attacked the United States of America. I hope that the destruction of lives, property and economy will not be in vain and that will unite all nations and bring world peace for generations to come. I hope that no future U. S. President will experience another disaster like this ever again.

Y. A.

Capitol Building Washington D.C. - Illustration by Maribel Soto

CONTENTS

GEORGE WASHINGTON   1

JOHN ADAMS   2

THOMAS JEFFERSON   3

JAMES MADISON   4

JAMES MONROE   5

JOHN QUINCY ADAMS   6

ANDREW JACKSON   7

MARTIN VAN BUREN   8

WILLIAM HENRY HARRISON   9

JOHN TYLER   10

JAMES K. POLK   11

ZACHARY TAYLOR   12

MILLARD FILLMORE   13

FRANKLIN PIERCE   14

JAMES BUCHANAN   15

ABRAHAM LINCOLN   16

ANDREW JOHNSON   17

ULYSSES S. GRANT   18

RUTHERFORD B. HAYES   19

JAMES A. GARFIELD   20

CHESTER A. ARTHUR   21

GROVER CLEVELAND   22

BENJAMIN HARRISON   23

GROVER CLEVELAND   24

WILLIAM McKINLEY   25

THEODORE ROOSEVELT   26

WILLIAM H. TAFT   27

WOODROW WILSON   28

WARREN G. HARDING   29

CALVIN COOLIDGE   30

HERBERT HOOVER   31

FRANKLIN D. ROOSEVELT   32

HARRY S. TRUMAN   33

DWIGHT D. EISENHOWER   34

JOHN F. KENNEDY   35

LYNDON B. JOHNSON   36

RICHARD M. NIXON   37

GERALD R. FORD   38

JIMMY CARTER   39

RONALD REAGAN   40

GEORGE BUSH   41

BILL CLINTON   42

GEORGE WALKER BUSH   43

A QUICK GUIDE TO THE U.S. PRESIDENTS   44-45

STATISTICS   46-48

PRESIDENTIAL OATH OF OFFICE   49

FAMOUS QUOTES   49

GETTYSBURG ADDRESS   50

BIBLIOGRAPHY   51

INDEX   52,53

George Washington

Wife and First Lady	Martha Dandridge Custis Washington
Number of Children	2 adopted children
Name of Children	John "Jack" Parke Custis - adopted
	Martha "Patsy" Custis - adopted
Father	Augustine Washington
Mother	Mary Ball Washington
Birthday and location	February 22, 1732, Westmoreland County, Virginia
Date of death and location	December 14, 1799, Mount Vernon, Virginia
Religion	Episcopalian
Political Party	Federalist
Term	April 30, 1789 to March 3,1797 (Two Terms)
Vice President	John Adams
Education	No formal education
Profession	Soldier, Statesman, surveyor, planter
Political career	• Member of Virginia House of Burgesses, 1759-74.
	• Member of Continental Congress, 1774-75.
	• Chairman of the Constitutional Convention, 1787-88.

Notable events

1783
• Treaty of Paris signed.

1789
• The Judiciary Act specified the number of Federal courts and judges.

1790
• Supreme Court met for the first time with John Jay as the Chief Justice.

1791
• A national banking system established by the Bank Act.
• The Bill of Rights took effect.

1792
• Post Office established by Congress as a separate entity.
• New York Stock Exchange organized.
• Regulating the Coins of the USA: Coinage Act.

1793
• The Proclamation of Neutrality during the war between England and France.

1794
• Whiskey Rebellion .

1795
• Treaty with Spain for Navigation opening the Mississippi River.

1796
Farewell Address.

John Adams

Wife and First Lady	Abigail Smith Adams
Number of Children	5 children
Name of Children	Abigail Amelia Adams
	John Quincy Adams
	Susanna Adams
	Charles Adams
	Thomas Boylston
Father	John Adams
Mother	Susanna Boylston Adams
Birthday and location	October 30, 1735, Braintree (Now Quincy), Massachusetts
Date of death and location	July 4, 1826, Quincy, Massachusetts
Religion	Unitarian
Political Party	Federalist
Term	March 4, 1797 to March 3, 1801 (One Term)
Vice President	Thomas Jefferson
Education	Graduated from Harvard College (1755)
Profession	Lawyer, diplomat, writer

Political career
- Member of Continental Congress, 1774-1778.
- Commissioner to France, 1778.
- Minister to the Netherlands, 1780.
- Minister to England, 1785.
- Vice President, 1789-97 (under Washington).

Notable events

1796
- E Pluribus Unum: "Out of Many, One"; added to American coins.

1797 - 1799
- Three anonymous French troublemakers brought France and the U.S. to the brink of war in what became known as the XYZ Affair.

1798
- Federalists support the highly unpopular Alien and Sedition Acts. They would later be repealed.

1799
- Fries Rebellion.

1800
- John and Abigail Adams were the first to move into the White House when the U.S. capital relocated to Washington, D.C. from Philadelphia.
- Jefferson defeated Adams in the election of 1801.
- Congress established Library of Congress.

1801
- Midnight Appointments.

Thomas Jefferson

Wife	Martha Wayles Skelton Jefferson
First Lady	Martha "Patsy" Randolph (daughter)
Number of Children	6
Name of Children	Martha Washington Jefferson Jane Randolph Jefferson Infant son (died before he was a month old) Mary Jefferson Lucy Elizabeth Jefferson Lucy Elizabeth Jefferson
Father	Peter Jefferson
Mother	Jane Randolph Jefferson
Birthday and location	April 13, 1743, Albemarle County, Virginia
Date of death and location	July 4, 1826, Charlottesville, Virginia
Religion	No specific denomination
Political Party	Democratic-Republican
Term	March 4, 1801 to March 3, 1809 (Two Terms)
Vice President	Aaron Burr (1st Term) George Clinton (2nd Term)
Education	Graduated from College of William and Mary (1762)
Profession	Lawyer, farmer, inventor, architect, statesman and writer

Political career
- Member of Virginia House of Burgesses, 1769-74.
- Member of Continental Congress, 1775-76.
- Governor of Virginia, 1779-81.
- Member of Continental Congress, 1783-85.
- Minister to France, 1785-89.
- Secretary of State, 1790-93 (under Washington).
- Vice President, 1797-1801 (under Adams).

Notable events

1801-1805
- Tripolitan War.
- **1803**
  Supreme Court ruled in *Marbury v. Madison* . Any law passed by Congress can be declared unconstitutional by the courts.
- The Louisiana Territory was purchased from France for three cents per acre for 512 million acres.

1804
- Presidential election rules changed by 12th Amendment .
- Jefferson reelected.
- Meriwether Lewis and William Clark began exploration of the Northwest.
- Vice President Aaron Burr kills Alexander Hamilton in a duel July 11.

1807
- Congress outlaws importing slaves from Africa, March 2.
- Embargo Act, December 22, forbids American ships to leave American waters.

1808
- Slave importation outlawed.

1809
- Non-Intercourse Act, repealed the Embargo Act.

James Madison

Wife and First Lady	Dolley Dandridge Payne Todd Madison
Number of Children	None
Name of Children	None
Father	James Madison
Mother	Nelly Rose Conway Madison
Birthday and location	March 16, 1751, Port Conway, Virginia
Date of death and location	June 28, 1836, Montpelier, Virginia
Religion	Episcopalian
Political Party	Democratic-Republican
Term	March 4, 1809 to March 3, 1817 (Two Terms)
Vice President	George Clinton (1st Term) Elbridge Gerry (2nd Term)
Education	Graduated from College of New Jersey (now Princeton University; 1771)
Profession	Lawyer
Political career	• Member of Virginia Constitutional Convention, 1776. • Member of Continental Congress, 1780-83. • Member of Virginia Legislature, 1784-86. • Member of Constitutional Convention, 1787. • Member of U.S. House of Representatives, 1789-97. • Secretary of State, 1801-09 (under Jefferson).
Notable events	**1787** • During the Constitutional Convention, Madison earned the title "Father of the Constitution". **1811** • Madison allows 20-year charter of Bank of the United States to lapse. • William Henry Harrison fought Indians led by Chief Tecumseh at Tippecanoe, near Indianapolis, November 7. **1812** • War declared on England on June 18 after England continued to attack U.S. ships headed to France. • Madison reelected. • Louisiana became the 18th state. **1814** • City of Washington captured and burned by British, August 24. • Treaty of Ghent ended War of 1812 on December 24, but fighting continued. **1816** • Second Bank of the United States chartered, April 10. • Indiana became the 19th state.

James Monroe

Wife and First Lady	Elizabeth Kortright Monroe
Number of children	3
Name of Children	Eliza Kortright Monroe James Spence Monroe Maria Hester Monroe
Father	Spence Monroe
Mother	Elizabeth Jones Monroe
Birthday and location	April 28, 1758, Westmoreland County, Virginia
Date of death and location	July 4, 1831, New York City, New York
Religion	Episcopalian
Political Party	Democratic-Republican
Term	March 4, 1817 to March 3, 1825 (Two Terms)
Vice President	Daniel D. Tompkins
Education	Graduated from College of William and Mary (1776)
Profession	Lawyer

Political career
- Member of Continental Congress, 1783-86.
- United States Senator, 1790-94.
- Minister to France, 1794-96.
- Governor of Virginia, 1799-1802.
- Minister to France and England, 1803-07.
- Secretary of State, 1811-17 (under Madison).
- Secretary of War, 1814-15 (under Madison).

Notable Events

1818
- Congress fixed the number of stripes on the U.S. flag at 13 to honor the original colonies, April 4.
- Anglo-American Convention set the 49th parallel as the border with Canada.

1819
- Florida ceded by Spain to the United States on February 22. In exchange the U.S. cancelled $5 million in Spanish debts.
- Panic of 1819.

1820
- The Missouri Compromise forbade slavery above 36 degrees, 30 minutes latitude.
- Monroe reelected.

1823
- On December 2, Monroe Doctrine delivered to Congress.

John Quincy Adams

Wife and First Lady	Louisa Catherine Johnson Adams
Number of Children	4
Name of Children	George Washington Adams John Adams Charles Francis Adams Louisiana Catherine Adams
Father	John Adams
Mother	Abigail Smith Adams
Birthday and location	July 11, 1767, Braintree (Now Quincy), Massachusetts
Date of death and location	February 23, 1848, Washington, D.C.
Religion	Unitarian
Political Party	Democratic-Republican
Term	March 4, 1825 to March 3, 1829 (One Term)
Vice President	John C. Calhoun
Education	Graduated from Harvard College (1787)
Profession	Lawyer

Political career

- Secretary to U.S. Minister to Russia, 1781.
- Minister to the Netherlands, 1794.
- Minister to Prussia, 1797-1801.
- United States Senator, 1803-08.
- Minister to Russia, 1809-11.
- Peace Commissioner at Treaty of Ghent, 1814.
- Secretary of State, 1817-25 (under Monroe).
- Member of U.S. House of Representatives, 1831-48.

Notable events

1825
- The appointment of Henry Clay as secretary of state, led to charges that the Clay and Adams made a bargain in the election of 1824.
- Erie Canal completed.

1826
- The Panama Congress.

1828
- Baltimore & Ohio railroad, the first designed for passengers and freight.
- Andrew Jackson defeated Adams.
- "Tariff of Abominations".

Andrew Jackson

Wife	Rachel Donelson Robards Jackson
First Lady	Emily Donelson (niece of wife Rachel)
Number of Children	1 adopted
Name of Children	Andrew Jackson Jr.
Father	Andrew Jackson
Mother	Elizabeth Hutchinson Jackson
Birthday and location	March 15, 1767, Waxhaw, South Carolina
Date of death and location	June 8, 1845, Nashville, Tennessee
Religion	Presbyterian
Political Party	Democratic
Term	March 4, 1829 to March 3, 1837 (Two Terms)
Vice President	John C. Calhoun (1st Term) Martin Van Buren (2nd Term)
Education	No formal education
Profession	Lawyer, soldier
Political career	• Member of U.S. House of Representatives, 1796-97. • United States Senator, 1797-98. • Justice on Tennessee Supreme Court, 1798-1804. • Governor of The Florida Territory, 1821. • United States Senator, 1823-25.
Notable Events	**1829** • Estate of James Smithson funded the establishment of the Smithsonian. • About 2,000 of Jackson's supporters given government jobs. Jackson also set up a "kitchen cabinet" of informal advisers. **1831** • Samuel F. Smith wrote "My Country, 'tis of Thee". **1832** • Jackson reelected. • South Carolina attempted to nullify federal tariff laws. Federal troops sent to South Carolina on December 10. **1835** • U.S. became debt free (briefly) for the only time in history. **1836** • 6000 Mexicans defeated 190 Americans in 12 days at the Alamo on March 6. • The Specie Circular ordered that gold and silver were the only currency acceptable for the purchase of federal lands, issued on July 11. • The Bank of the United States. • Spoils System.

Martin Van Buren

Wife	Hannah Hoes Van Buren
First Lady	Angelica Singleton Van Buren (daughter in law)
Number of Children	4
Name of Children	Abraham Van Buren
	John Van Buren
	Martin Van Buren
	Smith Thompson Van Buren
Father	Abraham Van Buren
Mother	Maria Goes Hoes Van Alen Van Buren
Birthday and location	December 5, 1782, Kinderhook, New York
Date of death and location	July 24, 1862, Kinderhook, New York
Religion	Dutch Reformed
Political Party	Democratic
Term	March 4, 1837 to March 3, 1841 (One Term)
Vice President	Richard M. Johnson
Education	Graduated from Kinderhook Academy (1796)
Profession	Lawyer

Political career
- New York State Senator, 1813-15.
- New York Attorney-General, 1815-19.
- United States Senator, 1821-29.
- Governor of New York, 1829.
- Secretary of State, 1829-1831 (under Jackson).
- Minister to England, 1831.
- Vice President, 1832-1837 (under Jackson).

Notable Events

1837
- Banks closed in Philadelphia and New York City on May 10. This was the beginning of the Panic of 1837. The depression that followed would last throughout Van Buren's term.

1838
- Trail of Tears. Thousands of Cherokee Indians forced from their homes in South and deported to Oklahoma.

1840
- William Henry Harrison defeated Van Buren.
- Second Seminole War.

William Henry Harrison

Wife	Anna Tuthill Symmes Harrison
First Lady	Jane Irwin Harrison (daughter-in-law)
Number of Children	10
Name of Children	Elizabeth Bassett Harrison
	John Cleves Symmes Harrison
	Lucy Singleton Harrison
	William Henry Harrison
	John Scott Harrison
	Benjamin Harrison
	Mary Symmes Harrison
	Carter Bassett Harrison
	Anna Tuthill Harrison
	James Findlay Harrison
Father	Benjamin Harrison
Mother	Elizabeth Bassett Harrison
Birthday and location	February 9, 1773, Berkeley, Virginia
Date of death and location	April 4, 1841, Washington, D.C.
Religion	Episcopalian
Political Party	Whig
Term	March 4, 1841 to April 4, 1841 (One Term)
Vice President	John Tyler
Education	University of Pennsylvania
Profession	Soldier
Political career	• Secretary of Northwest Territory, 1798.
	• Territorial Delegate to Congress, 1799-1801.
	• Territorial Governor of Indiana, 1801-13.
	• U.S. Congressman from Ohio, 1816-19.
	• United States Senator, 1825-28.
	• Minister to Colombia, 1828-29.
Notable Events	**1841**
	• Delivered the longest inaugural address on March 4. It was an extremely cold day and Harrison did not wear a hat while delivering the 105-minute speech. He contracted pneumonia and died in the White House one month later.

John Tyler

Wife	Letitia Christian Tyler
First Lady	Priscilla Cooper Tyler (daughter-in-law)
2nd Wife and First Lady	Julia Gardiner Tyler
Number of Children	15
Name of Children first marriage	Mary Tyler Robert Tyler John Tyler Letitia Tyler Elizabeth Tyler Anne Contesse Tyler Alice Tyler Tazewell Tyler
Name of Children second marriage	David Gardiner Tyler John Alexander Tyler Julia Tyler Lachlan Tyler Lyon Gardiner Tyler Robert Fitzwalter Tyler Pearl Tyler
Father	John Tyler
Mother	Mary Marot Armistead Tyler
Birthday and location	March 29, 1790, Charles City County, Virginia
Date of death and location	January 18, 1862, Richmond, Virginia
Religion	Episcopalian
Political Party	Whig
Term	April 6, 1841 to March 3, 1845 (One Term)
Vice President	None
Education	Graduated from the College of William and Mary (1807)
Profession	Lawyer
Political career	• Member of Virginia House of Delegates, 1811-16. • Member of U.S. House of Representatives, 1816-21. • Virginia State Legislator, 1823-25. • Governor of Virginia, 1825-26. • United States Senator, 1827-36. • Vice President, 1841 (under W.H. Harrison). • Member of Confederate States Congress, 1861-62.
Notable Events	**1841** • Tyler's cabinet resigned after he vetoed banking bills supported by the Whigs. • Preemption Act. **1844** • Far East opened to U.S. traders after a treaty with China signed: Treaty of Wanghia. **1845** • Annexation of Texas followed by war with Mexico.

James Knox Polk

Wife and First Lady	Sarah Childress Polk
Number of Children	None
Name of Children	None
Father	Samuel Polk
Mother	Jane Knox Polk
Birthday and location	November 2, 1795, Mecklenburg County, North Carolina
Date of death and location	June 15, 1849, Nashville, Tennessee
Religion	Presbyterian
Political Party	Democratic
Term	March 4, 1845 to March 3, 1849 (One Term)
Vice President	George M. Dallas
Education	**Graduated from the University of North Carolina (1818)**
Profession	Lawyer

Political career
- Member of Tennessee House of Representatives, 1823-25.
- Member of U.S. House of Representatives, 1825-39.
- Speaker of the House of Representatives, 1835-39.
- Governor of Tennessee, 1839-41.

Notable Events

1845
- Texas became the 28th State.

1846
- The War of Mexico .
- A large crack in the Liberty Bell - too large to permit the bell to be rung any more.
- Dispute with Britain over the Oregon Territory settled. Both nations get a part of the territory: Oregon Treaty.
- Walker Tariff.

1848
- Treaty of 1848 with Mexico gave the U.S. control over California, New Mexico, Arizona, Nevada, Utah and parts of Colorado and Wyoming.
- Gold discovered in California in December.

1849
- Creation of the Department of Interior.

Zachary Taylor

Wife	Margaret "Peggy" Mackall Smith Taylor
First Lady	Mary Elizabeth "Betty" Taylor Bliss (daughter)
Number of Children	6
Name of Children	Anna Margaret Mackall Taylor
	Sarah Knox Taylor
	Octavia Pannel Taylor
	Margaret Smith Taylor
	Mary Elizabeth Taylor
	Richard Taylor
Father	Lieutenant Colonel Richard Taylor
Mother	Sarah Dabney Strother Taylor
Birthday and location	November 24, 1784, Orange County, Virginia
Date of death and location	July 9, 1850, Washington, D.C.
Religion	Episcopalian
Political Party	Whig
Term	March 5, 1849 to July 9, 1850 (One Term)
Education	No formal education
Profession	Soldier
Political career	• None
Notable Events	**1850**

• The Clayton-Bulwer Treaty signed with Britain guaranteed that any future canal across Central America would be available to all nations.

Millard Fillmore

Wife and First Lady	Abigail Powers Fillmore
2nd Wife	Caroline Carmichael McIntosh Fillmore
Number of Children	2
Name of Children	Millard Powers Fillmore Mary Abigail Fillmore
Father	Nathaniel Fillmore
Mother	Phoebe Millard Fillmore
Birthday and location	January 7, 1800, Summerhill, New York
Date of death and location	March 8, 1874 , Buffalo, New York
Religion	Unitarian
Political Party	Whig
Term	July 10, 1850 to March 3, 1853 (One Term)
Vice President	None
Education	No formal education
Profession	Lawyer
Political career	• Member of New York State Assembly, 1828-31. • Member of U.S. House of Representatives, 1833-35. • Member of U.S. House of Representatives, 1837-45. • Comptroller of New York, 1847. • Vice President, 1849-1850 (under Taylor).
Notable Events	**1850** • Congress passed the Compromise of 1850 and Fugitive Slave Act in September. **1852 - 1854** • Perry's Mission to Japan.

Franklin Pierce

Wife and First Lady	Jane Means Appleton Pierce
Number of Children	3
Name of Children	Franklin Pierce Frank Robert Pierce Benjamin Pierce
Father	General Benjamin Pierce
Mother	Ann Kendrick Pierce
Birthday and location	November 23, 1804, Hillsborough (now Hillsboro), New Hampshire
Date of death and location	October 8, 1869, Concord, New Hampshire
Religion	Episcopalian
Political Party	Democratic
Term	March 4, 1853 to March 3, 1857 (One Term)
Vice President	William R.D. King (died April 18,1853 never performing official duties).
Education	Graduated from Bowdoin College (1824)
Profession	Lawyer, public official
Political career	• Served in New Hampshire Legislature, 1829-33. • Member of U.S. House of Representatives, 1833-37. • Unites States Senate, 1837-42.
Notable Events	**1853** • Gadsden Purchase. **1854** • Kansas-Nebraska Act . • Ostend Manifesto. • Treaty with Japan negotiated by Commodore Matthew Perry.

James Buchanan

Wife	Never married
First Lady	Harriet Lane (niece)
Number of Children	None
Name of Children	None
Father	James Buchanan
Mother	Elizabeth Speer Buchanan
Birthday and location	April 23, 1791, Cove Gap, Pennsylvania
Date of death and location	June 1, 1868, Lancaster, Pennsylvania
Religion	Presbyterian
Political Party	Democratic
Term	March 4, 1857 to March 3, 1861 (One Term)
Vice President	John C. Breckinridge
Education	Graduated from Dickinson College (1809)
Profession	Lawyer
Political career	• Member of Pennsylvania House of Representatives, 1815-16. • Member of U.S. House of Representatives, 1821-31. • Minister to Russia, 1832-34. • United States Senator, 1834-45. • Secretary of State, 1845-49 (under Polk). • Minister to England, 1853-56.
Notable Events	• He entered the White House at a time when the fight between North and South over slavery was spinning out of control, and both sides ignored his calls for compromise. • Panic of 1857 • Secession. In 1866 James Buchanan wrote the first published presidential memoir, "Mr. Buchanan's Administration on the Eve of the Rebellion", in part to justify his leadership and place in history.

Abraham Lincoln

Wife and First Lady	Mary Todd Lincoln
Number of Children	4
Names of children	Robert Todd Lincoln, Edward Baker Lincoln, William W. Lincoln, Thomas (Tad) Lincoln
Father	Thomas Lincoln
Mother	Nancy Hanks Lincoln
Birthday and location	February 12, 1809, Hodgenville, Hardin County, Kentucky
Date of death and location	April 15, 1865, Washington, D.C.
Political Party	Republican
Term	March 4, 1861 to April 15, 1865 (Two Terms)
Vice President	Hannibal Hamlin(1st term), Andrew Johnson (2nd term)
Education	No formal education
Profession	Lawyer
Political career	• Elected to Illinois State Legislature, 1834 • Member of U.S. House of Representatives, 1847-49.

Notable Events

1861-1865
• Secession.
• Civil War.
1862
• Homestead Act.
• Morrill Act.
• Establishment of Department of Agriculture.
1863
• National Banking System created.
• Emancipation Proclamation, freeing all slaves in the Confederate states.
• Lincoln delivered his most famous speech, the Gettysburg Address, on the site where over 50,000 men had lost their lives in the war's deadliest battle.
1864
• West Virginia became the 35th State.
• Nevada became the 36th State
1865
• Surrender of General Robert E. Lee.
• Actor John Wilkes Booth at Ford's Theater in Washington, D.C. shot Lincoln. The president died the following morning, throwing the nation into intense mourning, 1865.
•

Andrew Johnson

Wife	Eliza McCardle Johnson
First Lady	Martha Johnson Patterson (daughter)
Number of Children	5
Name of Children	Martha Johnson
	Charles Johnson
	Mary Johnson
	Robert Johnson
	Andrew Johnson
Father	Jacob Johnson
Mother	Mary McDonough Johnson
Birthday and location	December 29, 1808, Raleigh, North Carolina
Date of death and location	July 31, 1875, Carter's Station, Tennessee
Religion	No specific denomination
Political Party	Democratic
Term	April 15, 1865 to March 3, 1869 (One Term)
Vice President	None
Education	No formal education
Profession	Tailor, public official, legislator

Political career

- Served as Alderman of Greeneville, Tennessee, 1830-33.
- Elected Mayor of Greeneville, Tennessee, 1834.
- Member of Tennessee State Legislature, 1835-43.
- Member of U.S. House of Representatives, 1843-53.
- Governor of Tennessee, 1853-57.
- United States Senator, 1857-62.
- Military Governor of Tennessee, 1862-65.
- Vice President, 1865 (under Lincoln).
- United States Senator, 1875.

Notable Events

- Reconstruction .
- 1865 Thirteenth Amendment ratified
- Purchase of Alaska, 1867.
- Fourteenth Amendment ratified.
- Impeachment

Ulysses Simpson Grant

Wife and First Lady	Julia Boggs Dent Grant
Number of Children	4
Name of Children	Frederick Dent Grant
	Ulysses Simpson Grant
	Ellen "Nellie" Wrenshall Grant
	Jesse Root Grant
Father	Jesse Root Grant
Mother	Hannah Simpson Grant
Birthday and location	April 27, 1822, Point Pleasant, Ohio
Date of death and location	July 23, 1885, Mount McGregor, New York
Religion	Methodist
Political Party	Republican
Term	March 4, 1869 to March 3, 1877 (Two Terms)
Vice President	Schuyler Colfax (1st term)
	Henry Wilson (2nd term)
Education	Graduated from the U.S. Military Academy in West Point, N.Y. (1843)
Profession	Soldier
Political career	• None
Notable Events	**1869**

1869
• Junction of Pacific railroads and start of transcontinental service.
1870
• Creation of the Department of Justice.
• 15th Amendment ratified
1871
• Chicago fire.
1872
• Civil Service Act.
1873
• Financial crisis and panic.
1876
• Alexander Graham Bell invents the telephone.
• The Battle of Little Big Horn and death of General Custer.
• Colorado became the 38th State.
• Scandals: Members of the administration, including Grant's personal secretary, were involved in scams and bribery schemes that shocked the nation.
• Reconstruction

Rutherford Birchard Hayes

Wife and First Lady	Lucy Ware Webb Hayes
Number of Children	8
Name of Children	Birchard Austin Hayes
	James Webb Cook Hayes
	Rutherford Platt Hayes
	Joseph Thompson Hayes
	George Crook Hayes
	Fanny Hayes
	Scott Russell Hayes
	Manning Force Hayes
Father	Rutherford Hayes
Mother	Sophia Birchard Hayes
Birthday and location	October 4, 1822, Delaware, Ohio
Date of death and location	January 17, 1893, Fremont, Ohio
Religion	Methodist
Political Party	Republican
Term	March 4, 1877 to March 3, 1881 (One Term)
Vice President	William A. Wheeler
Education	Graduated from Kenyon College (1842) and Harvard Law School (1845)
Profession	Lawyer
Political career	• Member of U.S. House of Representatives, 1865-67.
	• Governor of Ohio, 1868-72.
	• Governor of Ohio, 1876-77.
Notable Events	**1877**
	• Federal troops withdrew from the South ending Reconstruction.
	• Striking railroad workers and federal troops clashed.
	1878
	• Bland-Allison Silver Purchase Act passed despite Hayes veto.
	1879
	• Resumption of the Specie Act.
	• Civil Service Reform.
	• The first president to use the telephone.

James Abram Garfield

Wife and First Lady	Lucretia Rudolph Garfield
Number of Children	7
Name of Children	Eliza Arabella Garfield
	Harry Augustus Garfield
	James Rudolph Garfield
	Mary "Molly" Garfield
	Irvin McDowel Garfield
	Abram Garfield
	Edward Garfield
Father	Abram Garfield
Mother	Eliza Ballou Garfield
Birthday and location	November 19, 1831, Orange, Ohio
Date of death and location	September 19, 1881, Elberon, New Jersey
Religion	Disciples of Christ
Political Party	Republican
Term	March 4, 1881 to September 19, 1881 (One Term)
Vice President	Chester A. Arthur
Education	Attended Western Reserve Eclectic Institute (now Hiram College); Graduated from Williams College (1856)
Profession	Teacher
Political career	• Member of Ohio State Senate, 1859-61.
	• Member of U.S. House of Representatives, 1863-80.
	• Elected to United States Senate, 1880.
Notable Events	• Victory over Republican Party Bosses.
	• Star Route Scandal.
	• Red Cross Initiated.
	1881
	• On July 2, shot by Charles Julius Guiteau. Garfield died of blood poisoning as a result of a gun wound on September 19.

Chester Alan Arthur

Wife	Ellen Lewis Herndon_Arthur
First Lady	Mary Arthur McElory (sister)
Number of Children	3
Name of Children	William Lewis Herndon Arthur
	Chester Alan Arthur
	Ellen Herndon Arthur
Father	William Arthur
Mother	Malvina Stone Arthur
Birthday and location	October 5, 1829, Fairfield, Vermont
Date of death and location	November 18, 1886, New York, New York
Religion	Episcopalian
Political Party	Republican
Term	September 19, 1881 to March 3, 1885 (One Term)
Vice President	None
Education	Graduated from Union College (1848)
Profession	Lawyer
Political career	• Vice president, 1881 (under Garfield).
Notable Events	• 1882 Chinese Exclusion Act
	• 1883 Pendleton Act
	• 1884 Establishment of territorial government in Alaska

Grover Cleveland

Wife and First Lady	Frances Folsom Cleveland
Number of Children	5
Name of Children	Ruth Cleveland
	Esther Cleveland
	Marion Cleveland
	Richard Falson Cleveland
	Francis Grover Cleveland
Father	Richard Folley Cleveland
Mother	Anne Neal Cleveland
Birthday and location	March 18, 1837, Caldwell, New Jersey
Date of death and location	June 24, 1908, Princeton, New Jersey
Religion	Presbyterian
Political Party	Democratic
Term	March 4, 1885 to March 3, 1889 and March 4, 1893 , to March 3, 1897 (Two Terms non-consecutive)
Vice President	Thomas A. Hendricks (1st Term)
	Adlai E. Stevenson (2nd Term)
Education	No formal education
Profession	Lawyer, Sheriff

Political career

- Sheriff of Erie County, NY, 1870-73.
- Mayor of Buffalo, NY, 1882.
- Governor of New York, 1883-85.

Notable Events

1886
- Dedication of the Statue of Liberty.
- Presidential Succession Act .
- Geronimo surrendered, ending Apache wars of New Mexico and Arizona.

1887
- Interstate Commerce Act.
- Anti-Polygamy Act.
- Dawes Severalty Act.
- Tenure of Office Act repealed.

1888
- New Chinese Exclusion Act.

1893
- Panic of 1893.
- 1894
- Pullman Strike.
- Sherman Silver Purchase Act of 1890 repealed.

1895
- Controversy with Great Britain over Venezuela.

Benjamin Harrison

Wife and First Lady	Caroline Lavinia Scott Harrison
2nd Wife	Mary Scott Lord Dimmick Harrison
Number of Children	3
Name of Children of first marriage	Russell Benjamin Harrison Mary Scott Harrison
Name of Children of second marriage	Elizabeth Harrison
Father	John Scott Harrison
Mother	Elizabeth Ramsey Irwin Harrison
Birthday and location	August 20, 1833, North Bend, Ohio
Date of death and location	March 13, 1901, Indianapolis, Indiana
Religion	Presbyterian
Political Party	Republican
Term	March 4, 1889 to March 3, 1893 (One Term)
Vice President	Levi P. Morton
Education	Graduated from Miami University (1852)
Profession	Lawyer
Political career	• United States Senator, 1881-87.
Notable Events	**1890** • Dependent and Disability Pensions Act. • Sherman Anti-Trust Act. • McKinley Tariff Act. **1891** Electricity installed in White House.

Grover Cleveland

Wife and First Lady	Frances Folsom Cleveland
Number of Children	5
Name of Children	Ruth Cleveland
	Esther Cleveland
	Marion Cleveland
	Richard Falson Cleveland
	Francis Grover Cleveland
Father	Richard Folley Cleveland
Mother	Anne Neal Cleveland
Birthday and location	March 18, 1837, Caldwell, New Jersey
Date of death and location	June 24, 1908, Princeton, New Jersey
Religion	Presbyterian
Political Party	Democratic
Term	March 4, 1885 to March 3, 1889 and March 4, 1893 to March 3, 1897 (Two Terms non-consecutive)
Vice President	Thomas A. Hendricks (1st Term)
	Adlai E. Stevenson (2nd Term)
Education	No formal education
Profession	Lawyer, Sheriff

Political career
- Sheriff of Erie County, NY, 1870-73.
- Mayor of Buffalo, NY, 1882.
- Governor of New York, 1883-85.

Notable Events

1886
- Dedication of the Statue of Liberty.
- Presidential Succession Act.
- Geronimo surrendered, ending Apache wars of New Mexico and Arizona.

1887
- Interstate Commerce Act.
- Anti-Polygamy Act.
- Dawes Severalty Act.
- Tenure of Office Act repealed.

1888
- New Chinese Exclusion Act .

1893
- Panic of 1893.
- 1894 Pullman Strike
- Sherman Silver Purchase Act of 1890 repealed
- 1895 Controversy with Great Britain over Venezuela.
-

William McKinley

Wife and First Lady	Ida Saxton McKinley
Number of Children	2
Name of Children	Katherine McKinley
	Ida McKinley
Father	William McKinley
Mother	Nancy Campbell Allison McKinley
Birthday and location	January 29, 1843, Niles, Ohio
Date of death and location	September 14, 1901,Buffalo, New York
Religion	Methodist
Political Party	Republican
Term	March 4, 1897 to September 14, 1901 (Two Terms)
Vice President	Garret A. Hobart (1st Term)
	Theodore Roosevelt (2nd Term)
Education	Attended Allegheny College
Profession	Lawyer
Political career	• Member of U.S. House of Representatives, 1877-91.
	• Governor of Ohio, 1892-96.

Notable Events

1898
• Annexation of Hawaii.
• Spanish-American War.
1899-1900
• Boxer Rebellion.
1901
During a visit to the Pan-American Exposition in Buffalo on September 6, an anarchist shot McKinley. Eight days later, he died.

Theodore Roosevelt

First Wife	Alice Hathaway Lee Roosevelt
2nd Wife and First Lady	Edith Kermit Carow Roosevelt
Number of Children	6
Name of Children of first marriage	Alice Lee Roosevelt
Name of Children of second marriage	Theodore Roosevelt Kermit Roosevelt Ethel Carow Roosevelt Archibald Bulloch Roosevelt Quentin Roosevelt
Father	Theodore Roosevelt
Mother	Martha Bullcoh Roosevelt
Birthday and location	October 27, 1858, New York, New York
Date of death and location	January 6, 1919, Oyster Bay, New York
Religion	Dutch Reformed Church
Political Party	Republican
Term	September 14, 1901 to March 3, 1909 (Two Terms)
Vice President	Charles W. Fairbanks
Education	Graduated from Harvard College (1880)
Profession	Rancher, writer, public official

Political career

- Member of New York State Assembly, 1882-84.
- Member of Civil Service Commission, 1889-95.
- Assistant Secretary of the Navy, 1895-97.
- Governor of New York, 1898-1900.
- Vice President, 1901 (under McKinley).

Notable Events

1904
- Issued an addition to the Monroe Doctrine in defense of U.S. intervention in Latin America to stop European aggressions.
- Panama Canal.

1906
- Federal Food and Drug Act.
- Roosevelt awarded Nobel Peace Prize for mediating peace between Russia and Japan, 1906.
- Conservation.

1907
- Oklahoma became the 46th State.
- The navigation of Great White Fleet US warships commanded by Rear Admiral Robley D. Evans and Charles S. Sperry.

1908
- Creation of the Bureau of Investigation (precursor to F.B.I.) for Department of Justice.

1909
- First narcotic prohibition act.

William Howard Taft

Wife and First Lady	Helen Herron Taft
Number of Children	3
Name of Children	Robert Alphonso Taft Helen Herron Taft Charles Phelps Taft
Father	Alphonso Taft
Mother	Louisa Maria Torrey Taft
Birthday and location	September 15, 1857, Cincinnati, Ohio
Date of death and location	March 8, 1930, Washington, D.C.
Religion	Unitarian
Political Party	Republican
Term	March 4, 1909 to March 3, 1913 (One Term)
Vice President	James S. Sherman
Education	Graduated from Yale College (1878); Cincinnati Law School (1880)
Profession	Lawyer, public official
Political career	• Judge in Ohio Superior Court, 1887-90. • U.S. Solicitor General, 1890-92. • U.S. Circuit Court Judge, 1892-1900 • Governor of the Philippines, 1901-04. • Secretary of War, 1904-08 (under T. Roosevelt). • Chief Justice of the U.S. Supreme Court, 1921-30.
Notable Events	**1912** • New Mexico became the 47th and Arizona the 48th State **1913,** • 16th Amendment ratified • Dollar Diplomacy.

Woodrow Wilson

Wife and First Lady	Ellen Louise Axson Wilson
2nd Wife and First Lady	Edith Bolling Galt Wilson
Number of Children	3
Name of Children of first marriage	Margaret Woodrow Wilson Jessie Woodrow Wilson Eleanor Randolph Wilson
Father	Joseph Ruggles Wilson
Mother	Jessie Janet Woodrow Wilson
Birthday and location	December 29 1856, Staunton, Virginia
Date of death and location	February 3, 1924, Washington, D.C.
Religion	Presbyterian
Political Party	Democratic
Term	March 4, 1913 to March 3, 1921 (Two Terms)
Vice President	Thomas R. Marshall
Education	Graduated from the College of New Jersey (now Princeton University) (1879);University of Virginia Law School(1881); Johns Hopkings University(1886)
Profession	Teacher, public official
Political career	• Governor of New Jersey, 1911-13.
Notable Events	**1913** • The Federal Reserve Act. • 17th Amendment. **1917-1918** • World War I, U.S. involvement. **1919** • 18th Amendment ratified, 14 points for World Peace. **1920** 19th Amendment.

Warren Gamaliel Harding

Wife and First Lady	Florence Kling De Wolfe Harding
Number of Children	None
Father	George Tyron Harding
Mother	Phoebe Elizabeth Dickerson Harding
Birthday and location	November 2, 1865, Corsica, Ohio
Date of death and location	August 2, 1923, San Francisco, California
Religion	Baptist
Political Party	Republican
Term	March 4, 1921 to August 2, 1923 (One Term)
Vice President	Calvin Coolidge
Education	Attended Ohio Central College
Profession	Editor-Publisher

Political career
• Member of Ohio State Senate, 1900-04.
• Lieutenant-Governor of Ohio, 1904-06.
• United States Senator, 1915-21.

Notable Events

1921
• Peace between Germany and Austria declared.
• Opposition to the League of Nations.
1922
• Beginning of the Teapot Dome Scandal
• Fordney-McCumber Tariff Act.
• Arms Limitation.

Calvin Coolidge

Wife and First Lady	Grace Anna Goodhue Coolidge
Number of Children	2
Name of Children	John Coolidge
	Calvin Coolidge
Father	John Calvin Coolidge
Mother	Victoria Josephine Moor Coolidge
Birthday and location	July 4, 1872, Plymouth, Vermont
Date of death and location	January 5, 1933, Northampton, Massachusetts
Religion	Congregationalist
Political Party	Republican
Term	August 3, 1923 to March 3, 1929 (Two Terms)
Vice President	Charles G. Dawes
Education	Graduated from Amherst College (1895)
Profession	Lawyer

Political career

- Northampton, MA City Councilman, 1899.
- City Solicitor, 1900-01.
- Clerk of Courts, 1904 .
- Member of Massachusetts Legislature, 1907-08.
- Mayor of Northampton, MA, 1910-11 .
- Member of Massachusetts Legislature, 1912-15 .
- Lieutenant-Governor of Massachusetts, 1916-18.
- Governor of Massachusetts, 1919-20 .
- Vice President, 1921-23 (under Harding).

Notable Events

1924
- Immigration Act.
1926   1927   . U.S. Radio Commission created
- Air Commerce Act.
1928
Kellogg-Briand Pact.

Herbert Clark Hoover

Wife and First Lady	Lou Henry Hoover
Number of Children	2
Name of Children	Herbert Clark Hoover
	Allan Henry Hoover
Father	Jesse Clark Hoover
Mother	Hulda Randall Minthorn Hoover
Birthday and location	August 10, 1874, West Branch, Iowa
Date of death and location	October 20, 1964, New York, New York
Religion	Society of Friends (Quaker)
Political Party	Republican
Term	March 4, 1929 to March 3, 1933 (One Term)
Vice President	Charles Curtis
Education	Graduated form Stanford University (1895)
Profession	Engineer
Political career	• Secretary of Commerce, 1921-23.
	• Secretary of Commerce, 1923-28.

Notable Events

1929
• Stock Market Crash.
• The Great Depression.
• 1931 " Star Spangled Banner" adopted as national anthem.
1933

Franklin Delano Roosevelt

Wife and First Lady	Anna Eleanor Roosevelt Roosevelt
Number of Children	6
Name of Children	Anna Eleanor Roosevelt James Roosevelt Franklin Roosevelt Elliott Roosevelt Franklin Delano Roosevelt John Aspinwall Roosevelt
Father	James Roosevelt
Mother	Sara Delano Roosevelt
Birthday and location	January 30, 1882, Hyde Park, New York
Date of death and location	April 12, 1945, Warm Springs, Georgia
Religion	Episcopalian
Political Party	Democratic
Term	March 4, 1933 to April 12, 1945 (Four Terms)
Vice President	John N. Garner (1933-1941) Henry A. Wallace (1941-1945) Harry S. Truman (1945)
Education	Graduated from Harvard College (1903); Attended Columbia Law School
Profession	Public official, lawyer
Political career	• Member of New York State Legislature, 1911-13. • Assistant Secretary of the Navy, 1913-20. • Governor of New York, 1929-33.
Notable Events	• New Deal. **1933** • 21st Amendment ratified. **1941-1945** • World War II and Great Depression. • Japan attacks Pearl Harbor, Roosevelt asked Congress to declare war.

Harry S. Truman

Wife and First Lady	Elizabeth "Bess" Virginia Wallace Truman
Number of Children	1
Name of Children	Margaret Truman
Father	John Anderson Truman
Mother	Martha Ellen Young Truman
Birthday and location	May 8, 1884, Lamar, Missouri
Date of death and location	December 26, 1972, Independence, City, Missouri
Religion	Baptist
Political Party	Democratic
Term	April 12, 1945 to January 20, 1953 (Two Terms)
Vice President	Alben W. Barkley
Education	Attended the University of Kansas City Law School
Profession	Farmer, public official, haberdasher.
Political career	• Judge on Jackson County Court, 1922-24.
	• Presiding Judge of Jackson County Court, 1926-34.
	• United States Senator, 1935-45.

Notable Events

1945
• Ending of World War II, (as President, he made the decision to drop the atom bomb on Hiroshima and Nagasaki).
• Formation of United Nations (U.N).

1947
• 22nd Amendment ratified.
• Truman Doctrine.
• Creation of C.I.A. (Central Intelligence Agency).

1948
• Formation of Organization of American States (O.A.S.).

1949
• Berlin blockade ended.
• NATO Pact.

1950
• Korean War.

Dwight David Eisenhower

Wife and First Lady	Mary "Mamie" Geneva Doud Eisenhower
Number or Children	2
Name of Children	Doud Dwight Eisenhower John Sheldon Doud Eisenhower
Father	David Jacob Eisenhower
Mother	Ida Elizabeth Stover Eisenhower
Birthday and location	October 14, 1890, Denison, Texas
Date of death and location	March 28, 1969, Washington, D.C.
Religion	Presbyterian
Political Party	Republican
Vice President	Richard M. Nixon
Term	January 20, 1953 to January 20, 1961 (Two Terms)
Education	Graduated from U.S. Military Academy, West Point, N.Y. (1915)
Profession	Army Officer, General, President of Columbia University.
Political career	• None

Notable Events

1953-1955
• Ending of Korean War.
• The Eisenhower Doctrine.
• Civil Rights - Established of Civil Rights Commission.
1954
• Supreme Court rules racial segregation in schools unconstitutional.
1956
• Interstate Highway System.
1957
• Federal troops sent to Little Rock, Ark. , to enforce integration of Black students.
1958
• Establishment of NASA.
1959
• Fidel Castro takes over Cuba.

John Fitzgerald Kennedy

Wife and First Lady	Jacqueline Lee Bouvier Kennedy
Number of Children	3
Name of Children	Caroline Bouvier Kennedy John Fitzgerald Kennedy, Jr. Patrick Bouvier Kennedy
Father	Joseph Patrick Kennedy
Mother	Rose Elizabeth Fitzgerald Kennedy
Birthday and location	May 29, 1917, Brookline, Massachusetts
Date of death and location	November 22, 1963, Dallas, Texas
Religion	Roman Catholic
Political Party	Democratic
Vice President	Lyndon B. Johnson
Term	January 20, 1961 to November 22, 1963 (One Term)
Education	Graduated from Harvard College (1940)
Profession	Author, public official
Political career	• Member of U.S. House of Representatives, 1947-53. • United States Senator, 1953-61.
Notable Events	**1961** • Bay of Pigs Invasion. • Established Peace Corps. **1962** • Cuban Missile Crisis. • U.S.A. Space Program. **1963** Shot by an assassin as his motorcade traveled through Dallas, Texas on November 22.

Lyndon Baines Johnson

Wife and First Lady	Claudia "Lady Bird" Alta Taylor Johnson
Number of Children	2
Name of Children	Lynda Bird Johnson
	Luci Baines Johnson
Father	Sam Ealy Johnson, Jr.
Mother	Rebekah Baines Johnson
Birthday and location	August 27, 1908, near Stonewall, Texas
Date of death and location	January 22, 1973, San Antonio, Texas
Religion	Disciples of Christ
Political Party	Democratic
Term	November 22, 1963 to January 20, 1969 (Two Terms)
Vice President	Hubert H. Humphrey
Education	Graduated from Southwest Texas State Teachers College (1930)
Profession	Teacher, public official

Political career

• Congressional Secretary, 1931-37.
• Member of U.S. House of Representatives, 1937-49.
• United States Senator, 1949-61.
• Vice President, 1961-63 (under Kennedy).

Notable Events

1964
• Civil Rights Act of 1964.
• War on Poverty .
1965
• First US combat troops (marines) in Vietnam.
• US Marines in Dominican Republic.
• Signed Medicare and Voting rights bill.
• Race riots in Los Angeles (Watts).
1966
• Department of Transportation
1967
• Expansion of US involvement in Vietnam War.
• Glassboro Summit between U.S. A.and U.S.S.R.
• Race riots in Newark, NJ and Detroit.
• **1968**
• Seizure by force of U.S.S. Pueblo by North Koreans
• Assassination of Dr. Martin Luther King Jr., and Senator Robert F. Kennedy.

Richard Milhous Nixon

Wife and First Lady	Thelma "Patricia" Catherine Ryan Nixon
Number of Children	2
Name of Children	Patricia "Tricia" Nixon Julie Nixon
Father	Francis Anthony Nixon
Mother	Hannah Milhous Nixon
Birthday and location	January 9, 1913, Yorba Linda, California
Date of death and location	April 22, 1994, New York City, New York
Religion	Quaker
Political Party	Republican
Vice President	Spiro T. Agnew (1st Term) Gerald R. Ford (2nd Term)
Term	January 20, 1969 to August 9, 1974 (Two Terms)
Education	Graduated from Whittier College (1934) and Duke University Law School (1937)
Profession	Lawyer, public official

Political career

- Attorney for U.S. Office of Emergency Management, 1942.
- Member of U.S. House of Representatives, 1947-51.
- United States Senator, 1951-53.
- Vice President, 1953-61 (under Eisenhower).

Notable Events

1969
- First man on the Moon.

1971
- Drastic fiscal and monetary policy to achieve economic stability.

1972-1974
- Watergate Scandal.

1972
- Strategic Arms Limitation.

1973
- Conclusion of Vietnam War - End of Military draft.
- Diplomatic opening to China.
- Energy crisis; mandatory fuel allocation.
- 4th Arab-Israeli War.

1974
- Creation of Federal Energy Administration.
- Resignation.

Gerald Rudolph Ford

Wife and First Lady	Elizabeth "Betty" Bloomer Warren Ford
Number of Children	4
Name of Children	Michael Gerald Ford
	John Gardner Ford
	Steven Meigs Ford
	Susan Elizabeth Ford
Father	Leslie Lynch King
Mother	Dorothy Ayer Gardner King Ford
Birthday and location	July 14, 1913, Omaha, Nebraska
Date of death and location	
Religion	Episcopalian
Political Party	Republican
Term	August 9, 1974 to January 20, 1977 (One Term)
Vice President	Nelson A. Rockefeller
Education	Graduated from the University of Michigan (1935) and Yale University Law School (1941)
Profession	Lawyer, public official
Political career	• Member of U.S. House of Representatives, 1949-73.
	• Vice President, 1973-74 (under Nixon).

Notable Events

1974
• Clemency for Vietnam Draft Evaders and Deserters.
• Unconditional pardon to President Nixon.
1975
• New York City Bail Out.Apollo/Soyuz space mission
• Extension of Voting Rights Act. The Mayaguez incident.
• Rescue of American and Vietnamese personnel and civilians in Saigon as the city fell to North Vietnamese.
• 1976
• Signing of Treaty to limit size of underground nuclear explosions, between U.S.S.R. and U.S.A.

James Earl Carter, Jr.

Wife and First Lady	Rosalynn Smith Carter
Number of Children	4
Name of Children	John William "Jack" Carter
	James Earl "Chip" Carter III
	Donnel Jeffrey "Jeff" Carter
	Amy Lynn Carter
Father	James Earl Carter
Mother	Lillian Gordy Carter
Birthday and location	October 1, 1924, Plains, Georgia
Date of death and location	
Religion	Baptist
Political Party	Democratic
Term	January 20, 1977 to January 20, 1981 (One Term)
Vice President	Walter F. Mondale
Education	Graduated from U.S. Naval Academy, (1946)
Profession	Farmer, public official,engineer, nuclear sub. commander
Political career	• Georgia State Senator, 1963-66.
	• Governor of Georgia, 1971-75.
Notable Events	**1977**
	• Panama Canal Treaty.
	1978
	• Camp David Accords.
	1979
	• Three Mile Island Accident.
	1979-1981
	American Hostages in Iran.

Ronald Wilson Reagan

Wife	Jane Wyman Reagan
2ⁿᵈ Wife and First Lady	Nancy Davis Reagan
Number of Children	4
Name of Children of first marriage	Maureen Elizabeth Reagan Michael Edward Reagan
Name of Children of second marriage	Patricia Ann Reagan Ronald "Skip" Prescott Reagan
Father	John Edward Reagan
Mother	Nelle Clyde Wilson Reagan
Birthday and location	February 6, 1911, Tampico, Illinois.
Date of death and location	
Religion	Episcopalian
Political Party	Republican
Term	January 20, 1981 - January 20, 1989 (Two Terms)
Vice President	George Bush
Education	Graduated from Eureka College (1932)
Profession	Actor, public official
Political career	• Governor of California - 1966 • Re-elected governor of California - 1970

Notable Events

1980
• John Hinckley shot Reagan. He made a remarkable recovery and went on to serve two terms.Release of Amer.hostages in
1982   **Iran.**
• First American President to address combined Houses of British Parliament.
1983
• Grenada Invasion.
1987 - 1988 Arms Control Pact with the Soviet Union

George Herbert Walker Bush

Wife and First Lady	Barbara Pierce Bush
Number of Children	6
Name of Children	George Walker Bush
	Robin Bush
	John Ellis "Jeb" Bush
	Neil Mallon Bush
	Marvin Pierce Bush
	Dorothy Pierce Bush
Father	Prescott Sheldon Bush
Mother	Dorothy Walker Bush
Birthday and location	June 12, 1924, Milton, Massachusetts
Date of death and location	
Religion	Episcopalian
Political Party	Republican
Term	January 20.1989 to January 20 1993 (One Term)
Vice President	J. Danforth Quayle
Education	Graduate from Yale University (1948)
Profession	Business man, Public Official

Political career
- Ambassador to the United Nations, 1971-72.
- Chairman of the Republican National Committee.
- Chief of the U.S. Liaison Office in the People's Republic of China.
- Director of the Central Intelligence Agency, 1976-77.
- Vice president under Ronald Reagan, 1980.

Notable Events

1989
- Savings and Loan Crisis.
- Withdrawal of Soviet troops from Afghanistan.

1998 - 1990
- Invasion of Panama.

1989 - 1991
- Destruction of Berlin Wall.

1990 - 1991
- Persian Gulf War

William Jefferson "Bill" Clinton

Wife and First Lady	Hillary Rodham Clinton
Number of Children	1
Name of Children	Chelsea Victoria Clinton
Father	William Jefferson Blythe III
Stepfather	Roger Clinton
Mother	Virginia Divine Blythe Clinton
Birthday and location	August 19, 1946, Hope, Arkansas
Date of death and location	
Religion	Baptist
Political Party	Democratic
Term	January 20, 1993 - January, 2001 (Two Terms)
Vice President	Albert A. Gore, Jr.
Education	Graduated from Georgetown University, (1968) and Yale University (1973). Rhodes Scholar, Oxford University.
Profession	Lawyer
Political career	• Attorney General of Arkansas, 1976 • Governor of Arkansas, 1978 -80 • Governor of Arkansas, 1982-92
Notable Events	• 1997 President Clinton and Congress agree to balance federal • budget by 2002 • Impeachment. • Monika Lewinsky affair. • First balanced budget since 1969 submitted by President Clinton for fiscal year 1999 **1998-1999 Kosovo**

George Walker Bush

Wife and First Lady	Laura Welch Bush
Number of Children	2
Name of Children	Barbara Pierce Bush Jenna Welch Bush
Father	George Herbert Walker Bush
Mother	Barbara Pierce Bush
Birthday and location	July 6, 1946, New Haven, Connecticut
Date of death and location	
Religion	Methodist
Political Party	Republican
Term	January 11, 2001 - Present
Vice President	Richard B. Cheney
Education	Graduated from Yale University (1968) and Harvard Business School (1975)
Profession	Business man, public official
Political career	• Governor of Texas, 1994-1998 • Re-elected governor of Texas - 1998-2000

Notable Events

2001
• Tax cuts.

 * Patient bill of rights
 * September 11, terrorists attack the U.S., President Bush
   declares war on terrorism throughout the world.
   -Specifically targets Osama bin Laden and his Al -Qaeda
   network , as well as the radical Taliban regime in Afghanistan.
   *Forms international coalition against terrorism.

44

A Quick Guide to the U.S. Presidents

President	Wife and/or First Lady	Date of Birth	Date of Death	Vice President	State Elected
George Washington (F) 1789-1797	Martha Dandridge C. Washington	Feb. 22, 1732	Dec.14, 1799	John Adams	Virginia
John Adams (F) 1797-1801	Abigail Smith Adams	Oct. 30, 1735	July 4, 1826	Thomas Jefferson	Massachusetts
Thomas Jefferson (DR) 1801-1809	Martha (Patsy) Randolph (daughter)	Apr. 13, 1743	July 4, 1826	Aaron Burr George Clinton (2nd T)	Virginia
James Madison (DR) 1809-1817	Dolley Payne Todd Madison	Mar. 16, 1751	June 28, 1836	George Clinton Elbridge Gerry (2nd T)	Virginia
James Monroe (DR) 1817-1825	Elizabeth Kortright Monroe	Apr. 28, 1758	July 4, 1831	Daniel D. Tompkins	Virginia
John Quincy Adams (DR) 1825-1829	Louisa Johnson Adams	July 11, 1767	Feb.23, 1848	John C. Calhoun	Massachusetts
Andrew Jackson (D) 1829-1837	Camily Donelson (nice of wife)	Mar. 15, 1767	June 8, 1845	John C. Calhoun Martin Van Buren (2nd T)	Tennessee
Martin Van Buren (D) 1837-1841	Angelica Singleton (daughter in law)	Dec. 5, 1782	July 24, 1862	Richard M. Johnson	New York
William Henry Harrison (W) 1841	Anna T. Symmes Harrison Jane Irwin Harrison (daughter in law)	Feb. 9, 1773	Apr. 4, 1841	John Tyler	Ohio
John Tyler (W) 1841-1845	Letitia Christian Tyler Julia Gardiner Tyler Priscilla Cooper Tyler (daughter in law)	Mar. 29, 1790	Jan, 18 1862	none	Virginia
James K. Polk (D) 1845-1849	Sarah Childress Polk	Nov. 2, 1795	June 15, 1849	George M. Dallas	Tennessee
Zachary Taylor (W) 1849-1850	Margaret Mackall Smith Taylor	Nov. 24, 1784	July 9, 1850	Millard Fillmore	Louisiana
Millard Fillmore (W) 1850-1853	Abigial Powers Fillmore	Jan. 7, 1800	Mar. 8, 1874	none	New York
Franklin Pierce (D) 1853-1857	Jane Means Appleton Pierce	Nov. 23, 1804	Oct. 8, 1869	William R. King	New Hampshire
James Buchanan (D) 1857-1861	Marriet Lane (nice)	Apr. 23, 1791	June 1, 1868	John C. Breckinridge	Pennsylvania
Abraham Lincoln (R) 1861-1865	Mary Todd Lincoln (wife)	Feb. 12, 1809	Apr. 15, 1865	Hannibal Hamlin Andrew Johnson	Illinois
Andrew Johnson (R) 1865-1869	Eliza McCardle Johnson (wife) Martha Johnson Patterson (first lady)	Dec. 29, 1808	July 31, 1875	none	Tennessee
Ulysses S. Grant (R) 1869-1877	Julia Dent Grant	Apr. 27, 1822	July 23, 1885	Schuyler Colfax Henry Wilson	Illinois
Rutherford B. Hayes (R) 1877-1881	Lucy Webb Hayes	Oct. 4, 1822	Jan. 17, 1893	William A. Wheeler	Ohio
James A. Garfield (R) 1881	Lucretia Rudolph Garfield	Nov. 19, 1831	Sep. 19, 1881	Chester A. Arthur	Ohio
Chester Arthur (R) 1881-1885	Ellen L. Arthur (wife) Mary Arthur Mc Elory (sister/first lady)	Oct. 5, 1829	Nov. 18, 1886	none	New York

President	Wife and/or First Lady	Date of Birth	Date of Death	Vice President	State Elected
Grover Cleveland 1885-1889	Frances Folsom Cleveland	Mar. 18, 1837	June 24, 1908	Thomas A. Hendricks	New York
Benjamin Harrison (R) 1889-1893	Caroline Scott Harrison	Aug. 20, 1833	Mar. 13, 1901	Levi P. Morton	Indiana
Grover Cleveland (D) 1893-1897	Frances Folsom Cleveland	Mar. 18, 1837	June 24, 1908	Adlai E. Stevenson	New York
William McKinley (R) 1897-1901	Ida Saxton McKinley	Jan. 29, 1843	Sep. 14, 1901	Garret A. Hobart Theodore Roosevelt	Ohio
Theodore Roosevelt (R) 1901-1909	Alice Hathaway Lee Roosevelt	Oct. 27, 1858	Jan. 6, 1919	Charles W. Fairbanks	New York
William Howard Taft (R) 1909-1913	Helen Herron Taft	Sep. 15, 1857	Mar. 8, 1930	James S. Sherman	Ohio
Woodrow Wilson (D) 1913-1921	Ellen Louise Axxon Wilson (1st wife) Edith Bolling Galt Wilson (2nd wife)	Dec. 28, 1856	Feb. 3, 1924	Thomas R. Marshall	New Jersey
Warren G. Harding (R) 1921-1923	Florence Kling De-Wolfe Harding	Nov. 2, 1865	Aug. 2, 1923	Calvin Coolidge	Ohio
Calvin Coolidge (R) 1923-1929	Grace Goodhue Coolidge	July 4, 1872	Jan. 5, 1933	Charles G. Dawes	Massachusetts
Herbert Hoover (R) 1929-1933	Lou Henry Hoover	Aug. 10, 1874	Oct. 20, 1964	Charles Curtis	California
Franklin D. Roosevelt (D) 1933-1945	Anna Eleanor Roosevelt Roosevelt	Jan. 30, 1882	Apr. 12, 1945	John N. Garner Henry Wallace Harry S. Truman	New York
Harry S. Truman (D) 1945-1953	Elizabeth Wallace Truman	May 8, 1884	Dec. 26, 1972	Alben W. Barkley	Missouri
Dwight D. Eisenhower (R) 1953-1961	Mary Doud Eisenhower	Oct. 14, 1890	Mar. 28, 1969	Richard M. Nixon	New York
John F. Kennedy (D) 1961-1963	Jacqueline Bouvier Kennedy	May 29, 1917	Nov. 22, 1963	Lyndon B. Johnson	Massachusetts
Lyndon B. Johnson (D) 1963-1969	Claudia Alta Taylor Johnson	Aug. 27, 1908	Jan. 22, 1973	Hubert H. Humphrey	Texas
Richard M. Nixon (R) 1969-1974	Thelma Catherine Ryan Nixon	Jan. 9, 1913	Apr. 22, 1994	Spiro T. Agnew Gerald R. Ford	New York California
Gerald R. Ford (R) 1974-1977	Elizabeth Bloomer Warren Ford	July 14, 1913		Nelson A. Rockefeller	Michigan
Jimmy Carter (D) 1977-1981	Rosalynn Smith Carter	Oct. 1, 1924		Walter F. Mondale	Georgia
Ronald Reagan (R) 1981-1989	Nancy Davis Reagan	Feb. 6, 1911		George W. Bush	California
George Bush (R) 1989-1993	Barbara Pierce Bush	June 12, 1924		J. Danforth Quayle	Texas
William J. Clinton (D) 1993-2001	Hillary Rodham Clinton	Aug. 19, 1946		Albert Gore, Jr.	Arkansas
George W. Bush (R) 2001-	Laura Welch Bush	July 6, 1946		Richard B. Cheney	Texas

STATISTICS

Names	Name of Presidents	Total
James	James Madison	6
	James Monroe	
	James Polk	
	James Buchanan	
	James Abram Garfield	
	James Earl Carter, Jr.	
John	John Adams	4
	John Quincy Adams	
	John Tyler	
	John F. Kennedy	
William	William Henry Harrison	4
	William McKinley	
	William Howard Taft	
	William Jefferson Clinton	
George	George Washington	3
	George Herbert Bush	
	George Walker Bush	
Franklin	Franklin Pierce	2
	Franklin D. Roosevelt	

Education	Name of Presidents	Total
No formal education	George Washington	7
	Andrew Jackson	
	Zachary Taylor	
	Millard Fillmore	
	Abraham Lincoln	
	Andrew Johnson	
	Grover Cleveland	
Harvard	John Adams	6
	John Quincy Adams	
	Rutherford Bichard Hayes	
	Theodore Roosevelt	
	Franklin D. Roosevelt	
	John Fitzgerald Kennedy	
Princeton University	James Madison	2
	Woodrow Wilson	
College of William and Mary	Thomas Jefferson	3
	James Monroe	
	John Tyler	
Yale	William Howard Taft	5
	Gerald Rudolph Ford	
	George Bush	
	Bill Clinton	
	George W. Bush	

Occupation	Name of Presidents	Total
Soldier	George Washington	6
	Andrew Jackson	
	William Henry Harrison	
	Zachary Taylor	
	Ulysses Simpson Grant	
	Dwight David Eisenhower	
Lawyer	John Adams	26
	Thomas Jefferson	
	James Madison	
	James Monroe	
	John Quincy Adams	
	Andrew Jackson	
	Martin Van Buren	
	John Tyler	
	James Knox Polk	
	Millard Fillmore	
	Franklin Pierce	
	James Buchanan	
	Abraham Lincoln	
	Rutherford Bichard Hayes	
	Chester Alan Arthur	
	Grover Cleveland	
	Benjamin Harrison	
	William McKinley	
	Theodoro Roosevelt	
	William Howard Taft	
	Woodrow Wilson	
	Calvin Coolidge	
	Franklin D. Roosevelt	
	Richard Nixon	
	Gerald Ford	
	Bill Clinton	
Writer / Author	Thomas Jefferson	3
	Theodore Roosevelt	
	John F. Kennedy	
Public Official	Franklin Pierce	14
	Andrew Johnson	
	James Abram Garfield	
	Theodore Roosevelt	
	William Taft	
	Woodrow Wilson	
	Franklin D. Roosevelt	
	Harry S. Truman	
	John F. Kennedy	
	Lyndon Johnson	
	Richard Nixon	
	Gerald Ford	
	James Earl Carter, Jr.	
	George Bush	

Occupation	Name of Presidents	Total
Farmer	Harry S. Truman James Earl Carter, Jr.	2
Teacher	Chester Alan Arthur Woodrow Wilson Lyndon Johnson	3
Business Man	George Bush George W. Bush	2

Birthday places	Name of Presidents	Total
Virginia	George Washington ,Thomas Jefferson ,James Madison,James Monroe, William H. Harrison ,John Tyler,Zachary Taylor, Woodrow Wilson	8
Ohio	Ulysses Grant, Rutherford Hayes ,James Garfield,Benjamin Harrison McKinley ,William Taft, Warren G. Harding	7
New York	Martin Van Buren , Millard Fillmore ,Theodore Roosevelt ,Franklin Roosevelt	4
Massachusetts	John Adams ,John Quincy Adams, John F. Kennedy, George Bush	4
North Carolina	James K. Polk,Andrew Johnson	2
Texas	Dwight D. Eisenhower , Lyndon B. Johnson	2
Vermont	Chester A. Arthur, Calvin Coolidge	2
Arkansas	William Clinton	1
California	Richard Nixon	1
Georgia	James Carter	1
Illinois	Ronald Reagan	1
Iowa	Herbert Hoover	1
Kentucky	Abraham Lincoln	1
Missouri	Harry Truman	1
Nebraska	Gerald Ford	1
New Hampshire	Franklin Pierce	1
New Jersey	Grover Cleveland	1
Pennsylvania	James Buchanan	1
South Carolina	Andrew Jackson	1
Connecticut	George W. Bush	1

I do solemnly swear (or affirm) that I will faithfully execute the Office of Presidents of the United States, and will to the best of my ability, preserve, protect and defend the constitution of the United States.

***

Famous Quotes

We the General Assembly of Virginia do enact that no man shall be compelled to frequent or support any religious worship, place, or ministry whatsoever, nor shall be enforced, restrained, molested, or burthened in his body or goods, or shall otherwise suffer, on account of his religious opinions or belief; but that all men shall be free to profess, and by argument to maintain, their opinions in matters of religion, and that the same shall in no wise diminish, enlarge, or affect their civil capacities.

*The bill drawn up by Thomas Jefferson establishing
Religious freedom in Virginia, 1779*

***

*"The only thing we have to fear is fear itself"
Franklin D. Roosevelt*

***

Let the word go from this time and place, to friend and foe alike, that the torch has been passed to a new generation of Americans...Let every nation know, whether it wishes us well or ill, that we shall pay any price, bear any burden, meet any hardship, support any friend, oppose any foe to assure the survival and the success of liberty ....If a free society can not help the many who are poor, it cannot save the few who are rich... All this will not be finished in the first one hundred days. Nor will it be finished in the first one thousand days, nor in the life of this Administration, nor even perhaps in our lifetime on this planet. But let us begin.
....And so, my fellow Americans: ask not what your country can do for you-ask what you can do for your country.

*President John F. Kennedy
January 20th, 1961*

***

LINCOLN'S GETTYSBURG ADDRESS

Delivered on November 19, 1863, this speech by President Lincoln commemorated the battle fought at Gettysburg July 1-3, 1863:

"Fourscore and seven years ago our fathers brought forth on this continent a new nation, conceived in liberty, and dedicated the proposition that all men are created equal.

Now we are engaged in a great civil war, testing whether that nation, or any nation so conceived and so dedicated, can long endure. We are met on a great battlefield of that war. We have come to dedicate a portion of that field as a final resting place for those who here gave their lives that the nation might live. It is altogether fitting and proper that we should do this.

But, in a larger sense we cannot dedicate-we cannot consecrate-we cannot hallow-this ground. The brave men, living and dead, who struggled here, have consecrated it far above our poor power to add or detract. The world will little note nor long remember what we say here, but it can never forget what they did here. It is for us, the living, rather, to be dedicated here to the unfinished work which they who fought here have thus far so nobly advanced. It is rather for us to be here dedicated to the great task remaining before us-that from these honored dead we take increased devotion to that cause for which they gave the last full measure of devotion; that we here highly resolve that these dead shall not have died in vain; that this nation under God, shall have a new birth of freedom; and the government of the people, by the people, for the people, shall not perish from the earth."

***

BIBLIOGRAPHY

51

- Biography.com (http://www.biography.com)
- C-SPAN. Presidential Fact Cards, Brief life stories of all presidents, 1999.
- Grolier.com. The American Presidency. (http://gi.grolier.com/presidents/preshome.html). Grolier 2000
- Joseph Nathan Kane. Presidential Fact Book. Random House, Inc. New York, 1998
- Krull Kathleen. Lives of the Presidents, Fame , Shame (and What the Neighbors Thought). Harcourt Brace & Company, 1998.
- Kunhardt, Philip and Peter, The American Presidents, Putnam Penguin.
- Summers, Robert S. "POTUS: Presidents of the United States" Internet Public Library, 2001. (http://www.ipl.org/ref/POTUS/)

INDEX

A QUICK GUIDE TO U.S. PRESIDENTS	44,45
ADAMS JOHN	2
ADAMS JOHN QUINCY	6
ARTHUR CHESTER ALAN	21
BIBLIOGRAPHY	51
BUCHANAN JAMES	15
BUSH GEORGE HERBERT WALKER	41
BUSH GEORGE WALKER	43
CARTER JIMMY	39
CLEVELAND GROVER	22,24
CLINTON WILLIAM JEFFERSON (BILL)	42
COOLIDGE CALVIN	30
EISENHOWER DWIGHT DAVID	34
FILLMORE MILLARD	13
FORD GERALD RUDOLPH	38
GARFIELD JAMES ABRAM	20
GRANT ULYSSES SIMPSON	18
GETTYSBURG ADDRESS	50
HARDING WARREN GAMALIEL	29
HARRISON BENJAMIN	23
HARRISON WILLIAM HENRY	9
HAYES RUTHERFORD BIRCHARD	19
HOOVER HERBERT CLARK	31
JACKSON ANDREW	7
JEFFERSON THOMAS	3
JOHNSON ANDREW	17
JOHNSON LYNDON BAINES	36
KENNEDY JOHN FITZGERALD	35
LINCOLN ABRAHAM	16
MCKINLEY WILLIAM	25
MADISON JAMES	4
MONROE JAMES	5
NIXON RICHARD M.	37
PIERCE FRANKLIN	14
POLK JAMES KNOX	11
PRESIDENTIAL OATH OF OFFICE	49
REAGAN RONALD WILSON	40
ROOSEVELT FRANKLIN DELANO	32

ROOSEVELT THEODORE   26
STATISTICS   46-48
TAFT WILLIAM HOWARD   27
TAYLOR ZACHARY   12
TRUMAN HARRY   33
TYLER JOHN   10
VAN BUREN MARTIN   8
WASHINGTON GEORGE   1
WILSON WOODROW   28

DIRECTORY OF AMERICAN PRESIDENTS: Is a compilation of data about their wives, children, birth and death dates and party, term, education, occupation and notable events during the terms of 43 U.S. Presidents. This directory has data about their places of birth, colleges attended, occupation and first names. This book is intended for students, history buffs, trivia and game show contestants. It also includes a picture of George Washington's Inauguration, illustrations of the Capitol Building , Jefferson Memorial and the White House, as well as the Gettysburg Address, presidential oath and famous quotations. It is intended to function as a source of quick reference, providing brief information about important events of presidents' lives during their terms of service.

It is a must for students of all ages, trivia and game show contestants .

Revised after the tragic events of September 11, 2001.

This book can be ordered by mail from the publisher:

Woodside House

P.O.Box 750217

Forest Hills,N.Y. 11375

Visit us on the web

www.woodsidehouse.net